Explosive Combat
Wing Chun

Volume One

EXPLOSIVE COMBAT
WING CHUN

Volume One

SIFU ALAN LAMB

UNIQUE PUBLICATIONS
Burbank, California

Disclaimer

Please note that the author and publisher of this book are NOT RESPONSIBLE in any manner whatsoever for any injury that may result from practicing the techniques and/or following the instructions given within. Since the physical activities described herein may be too strenuous in nature for some readers to engage in safely, it is essential that a physician be consulted prior to training.

First published in 2002 by Unique Publications.

Library of Congress Catalog Number: 2002015355
ISBN: 0-86568-208-9

Unique Publications
4201 Vanowen Place
Burbank, CA 91505
(800) 332–3330
First edition
05 04 03 02 01 00 99 98 97 1 3 5 7 9 10 8 6 4 2

Printed in the United States of America

Editor: John S. Soet
Design: Patrick Gross
Cover Design: George Chen

DEDICATION

This book is dedicated to the memory of John White, paratrooper-lumberjack-martial artist-mentor and all around good guy. He was a positive influence when I was young and not so wise. Everyone needs an Uncle John!

ACKNOWLEDGEMENTS

First, I wish to thank Koo Sang Sifu for sharing his knowledge of Wing Chun. Also, Sifu Paul Lam and Sifu Joseph Cheng for giving me a sound foundation in the art of Wing Chun Kung-Fu. Thanks to my students and friends who participated in demonstrating the techniques. Special thanks and appreciation goes to Lori Abril for her support, encouragement, and strong organizational skills. And last but not least to Jose Fraguas and C.F.W. Enterprises for publishing this work.

About the Author

Alan Lamb is England's first Hong Kong trained Master of Wing Chun. He has been involved in the martial arts for over 30 years, beginning first with the Wado Ryu style of Karate, and later turning to Wing Chun Kung-Fu, which he has practiced for over twenty-five years. For several years he studied in London under Sifu Paul Lam, a prominent teacher of Wing Chun in England. Later he studied with Sifu Joseph Cheng, also in London. Subsequently, he was accepted for a year long instructor's course in Hong Kong under Master Koo Sang, a direct disciple of Yip Man, the Grand Master of Wing Chun Kung-Fu. During his stay in Hong Kong, Malaysia and Singapore, Lamb also studied some miscellaneous aspects of the Siu Lum Ji with Sifu Wong Wan Chin, a Shaolin monk. Later, he studied Filipino martial arts with several teachers, including Professor Vee of New York.

In 1974 Lamb graduated from Mr. Koo's academy and earned the title Sifu ("teacher") of Wing Chun Kung-Fu.

He later established schools in both England and the United States and is presently teaching a select group of students in California.

Sifu Lamb is also concentrating on promoting the art of Wing Chun through movies and television. He has demonstrated his art in England, Hong Kong, the United States, and Latin America, as well as making a special guest appearance in "The Oriental World of Self Defense" at Madison Square Garden.

Anyone who is interested in studying personally with Sifu Lamb can contact him through the publishers.

CONTENTS

Introduction

Hello and welcome to my first volume on the "Explosive Combat Wing Chun" Series for C.F.W. Enterprises. My goal in writing this informative analysis of Wing Chun for combat is to present the art in a way that everyone can understand it, regardless of style or prior training in the martial arts.

This book is not meant to be a substitute for a competent teacher, but rather a guide for those interested in studying and applying the art of Wing Chun Kung-Fu.

Recently there have been some new theories regarding the origins of Wing Chun. Some teachers have created controversy by stating the story of Yim Wing Chun was merely a legend, no more than a Chinese fairy tale. However, I personally believe that whatever their role, women were involved in the development of Wing Chun. To that end I have included one of my favorite stories on the origins of Wing Chun.

Good luck with your training and I wish you success in your study of the art of "Explosive Combat Wing Chun."

—Alan Lamb
Burbank, California 2001

The Legend of Wing Chun

There are many intriguing stories as to the origins of Wing Chun. I would like to give one of the more popular versions of the Wing Chun legend as told to me by people in Hong Kong who claimed to be historians of the classical martial arts.

Some four hundred years ago, five famous teachers of the martial arts left the Fukien Shaolin Temple to spread the famous fighting techniques of the Shaolin Monks. One of these teachers was a woman called Ng Mui. She spread her own brand of Shaolin Kung-Fu, called Ng Mui Pai, throughout southeast Asia. After many years of active teaching, Ng Mui "closed her hands," a phrase the Chinese use to mean that a teacher has gone into retirement. During her years of inactivity, Ng Mui contemplated much on the principles of Kung-Fu and decided that much of what she had learned was too hard and too rigid, and that many of the stances and basic positions were too low and strength-oriented, making it difficult for people with limited time to gain any short-term benefits from Kung-Fu training. She began to shorten the "forms" or "classical sets" of Kung-Fu, eliminating needless repetition of unessential movements until day by day she came closer to perfecting a more efficient fighting art. One day as she was walking through a garden, she saw a hawk fighting with a snake. The hawk would try and grab the snake with its claw and peck with its beak. The snake however would curl and twist making it difficult for the hawk to get a good grip on its body. The snake would always manage to wiggle free from the hawk's grasp and bite back. This caused the hawk to release and ward off the attack with its wing. The actions of these two animals prompted Ng Mui to devise the Lap Sau, "Warding off Hands," which entails using the Wing Block to deflect an attack, as well as the Chi Sau, or "Sticking Hands," the most important part of Wing Chun training.

In the same village that Ng Mui lived was a young girl called Yim Wing Chun, which literally means "Beautiful Springtime." Her mother had just died and she was being annoyed by the local bully, a rogue boxer of the Eagle Claw school, who wanted to marry her. Although Yim Wing Chun had studied the fundamentals of Shaolin Kung-Fu from her father, she knew she would be no match for the bully if she tried to resist him, and so she sought out Ng Mui to ask her advice. During this time, under Chinese law, if a girl's mother died, she could not marry for three hundred days. Ng Mui told Yim Wing Chun to tell the bully that she would fight him after three hundred days and if he won she would marry him, but if she won, she would be free to marry whomever she wished. The bully readily agreed because he felt that no woman would be able to match his martial arts skills.

Yim Wing Chun began studying with Ng Mui, learning the new form of Kung-Fu that she had devised. She was an eager student and after three hundred days became extremely adept. On the day of the contest the bully strode in and arrogantly assumed a classical Horse Stance. But before he could move, Yim Wing Chun stepped forward at lightning speed and hit him in the face with a flurry of telling punches that knocked him to the ground. Enraged, he jumped up and immediately assumed an aggressive pose ready for the attack. Yim Wing Chun begged him to reconsider and to end the contest but he launched a fierce attack upon the girl. Before his hands could reach her, she knocked them up by slapping hard under both of his elbows, and, at the same time, drove a front kick up under his heart, killing him.

Yim Wing Chun then resumed her training with Ng Mui and perfected the Chi Sau techniques. She developed the three basic forms of the system, the Siu Lum Tau, Cham Kiu, and Biu Jee, and incorporated the sets of training on the Wooden Dummy or "Mok Jong." Later she married a teacher of Kung-Fu, Learng Bok Cho, who added the Butterfly Knives and Long Pole sets to the system. Both Yim Wing Chun and her husband then both began teaching this new art which soon took the name of Wing Chun Kung-Fu.

WING CHUN BASICS

Breathing

Breath control is one of the most basic, but important aspects of all systems of Kung-Fu and, hence, is a critical aspect learning Wing Chun. Breath control is performed in Wing Chun by focusing on the lower abdomen, in the region of the "Tan Tien," which is just below the navel. Breathing should be deep, but relaxed, with the tip of the tongue fixed just above the front teeth, the lips slightly parted. Normal inhalation and exhalation is performed through the nose. However, at the end of each formal exercise, one releases the tongue and gently exhales through the mouth.

Basic Stance Work

Just as a house needs a firm foundation before the builder can safely add the upper floors, so too a practitioner of Kung-Fu needs a firm foundation, with strong legs, before he can build the upper body defenses. Wing Chun is unique among Kung-Fu styles, because in the beginning stages, only two stances are used from which all the basic techniques are learned and applied from:

1. The parallel stance
2. The turning stance
3. The fighting stance
4. Basic footwork. Sliding stance.

Basic Punching

In Wing Chun the best defense is often said to be an aggressive offense. Many Wing Chun practitioners prefer to use deflection punches and risk being hit, just to be certain of making contact with an attacker's arms, so they can land a knockout or telling blow on their attacker.

1. The Wing Chun Center Line Thrusting Punch

⋏ Center Line Punching.
Place the left hand approximately one fist distance from the chest.

⋏ Punch out at nose level with a vertical first.

⋏Place right hand in guarding position.

⋏The right hand punches over the left in a straight line, as the left hand assumes a rear guarding position.

⋖Now, the left hand punches over the right in a continuous pattern. One hand punching, the other hand guarding. In the beginning, practice about 50 to 100 repetitions. Always begin punching slowly, so as not to injure the elbows.

2. Inside Punching

Example of the "Inside Punch"

⋀Ryan attacks with a straight left punch.

⋀Sifu Lamb prepares to counterpunch.

⋀Sifu Lamb "straight blasts" down the center line.

⋀Completion of the counterstrike.

3. Outside Punching

Example of the "Outside Punch"

⋏Sifu Lamb prepares to throw his punch over the attacking arm.

⋏Ryan attacks with a straight left punch.

⋏Sifu Lamb's punch suppresses Ryan's punch from the "outside as the punch slams into Ryan's ribs. Lamb's punch suppresses and attacks all in one motion.

4. Chain Punching
Chain Punching Exercise

⋏Face your partner in a "square" stance with left forearms crossed.

⋏Begin by counterpunching in a "punch" for "punch" motion using the straight punch.

⋏Build up to 100 reps per set.

⋏Use this drill to build forward energy and "bridging" power.

5. Pivot Punching

◁ Begin by opening stance in "classic" Wing Chun fashion. Raise both arms into double palm-up block and sink the breath into the lower abdomen.

➢ Bend both knees.

◁ Turn both feet out by pivoting on the heels.

➢ Rotate both heels out, sink the breath by tilting the pelvis forward. Squeeze both knees inward by contracting the leg adductor muscles.

◄ Assume left "square" guarding stance.

➤ Pivot stance to the right and thrust out at nose level with a straight left punch.

◄ 99 Drop fists to "midline" position.

➤ Pivot stance to the left and chamber a right punch.

◁Thrust out at nose level with straight right punch.

➢ Sink elbows for protection and again drop fists to "midline" position.

◁Repeat sequence and quickly pivot left and right sides, throwing alternate pivot punches. Build up to about 50 to 100 reps on each side.

6. Slide Step Punching

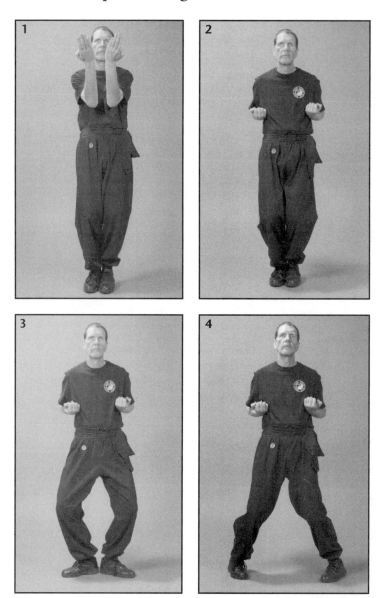

⚤ Open stance in "classic" Wing Chun fashion as shown in photos 1–4.

⋏Assume left guarding position.

⋏Pivot on heels smoothly into left guarding stance.

⋏Turn 180° to the right by pivoting on the heels into right guarding stance.

➤Practice pivoting into left and right guarding positions until the technique becomes quick and fluid. Remember, left and right sides should be "mirror" opposites of each other.

Slide Step Punch Example

◄ Assume left guarding stance.

➤ Slide forward by "pushing off" from the rear leg as you chamber the right punch.

◄ Thrust out at "nose" level with right punch, breathing naturally.

➤ Sink left elbow for protection.

◁ Slide forward and thrust out at "nose" level with left punch.

➤ Repeat up to 10 times.

◁ Sink right elbow for protection.

➤ Begin turning to the right.

◁ Pivot into right stance.

➢ Slide forward into straight left punch.

◁ Drop elbow for protection.

➢ Slide forward into right straight punch.

△ Drop elbow for protection.　　　　　　△ Repeat up to 10 times.

◁ Turn back into "square" stance.

◁ Draw back both fists into high rear chambered position.

➤ Point right foot forward.

◁ Bring left foot to right so feet are together

➤ Straighten both legs. As you press down with both palms, exhale to finish sequence.

7. Snap Punching

◁Snap punching is simply allowing the punching arm's elbow to sink back into a defensive position after a straight left punch.

➤Elbow quickly snaps back.

◁A right thrust punch.

➤The elbow quickly snaps back. Repeat the snap punching 50 to 100 reps on each side. This exercise builds up elbow power and the ability to strike hard from close-range. Think of Bruce Lee's famous "one inch" and "three inch" punches to visualize the power of snap

punching. Punching with light weights will greatly increase punching power. However, remember to punch an equal number of reps without weights. Otherwise, you will get too "tight." Flexible power is important for Wing Chun training. Keep "loose!"

Basic Kicks

Most basic kicks in Wing Chun are delivered from the forward or lead leg. Although Wing Chun uses the same kind of kicks as other styles, they are usually applied lower so that the hands can be used to block and counter attack. Stance work for kicking is developed by standing on one leg, which helps to build rooting and balance. Later, the kicks are further developed through the advanced drill called Chi Gerk, which is the Wing Chun art of "Sticking Legs."

The five basic kicks as well as the one-legged training position are as follows:

1. Shin Kick
2. Groin Kick
3. Front Kick
4. Side Kick
5. Round Kick
6. One Leg Standing position

Shin Kick

[Although most Wing Chun kicks are executed from the forward leg, it is important to practice kicks in the forward and rear leg on both the left and right sides. Only the right side is shown here but you must develop the ability to kick with either leg and from any position.]

◁Assume right leg forward guarding position.

➢Draw knee upwards and turn toes to the right.

◁Stomp down with the heel at knee or shin level.

➢Return leg to right guarding position.

Groin Kick

◁ Right guarding position.

➤ Draw right knee upwards and point toes straight down.

◁ Kick out with top of the foot at groin level.

➤ With a snapping motion, return the foot to right guarding position.

Front Heel Kick

◁ Assume right guard-
ing position.

➤ Draw knee
upwards.

◁ Kick out with
the heel at stomach
or chest level.

➤ Quickly return foot
to right guarding
position.

Side Kick

◁Assume right guard-
ing position.

➤Draw right knee
upwards and lower
right arm into a low
Wing Block position.

◁Pivot and thrust out with heel at waist level.

➤Quickly
return
to right
guarding
position.

Round Kick

◀Assume right guarding position.

▶Draw right knee upwards and point toes straight down

◀With a circular motion kick out with instep to the body.

▶Quickly return to right guarding position.

Basic Blocking

The Basic Wing Chun Defense Zones or "The Four Gates"
The basic blocking drills teach you how to protect the four gates. The four gates are defined by drawing a vertical line down the center of the body and a horizontal line at the elbow level. (See Photos).

Blocking Drill No. 1

⋏ Begin the blocking exercises by facing each other in a square stance.

⋏ Start with the left hand, palm-up. Block the arm crossing at the wrists. Apply forward pressure as you block out.

⋏ Snap arm down into a palm-down block.

⋏ Then return to the palm-up block.

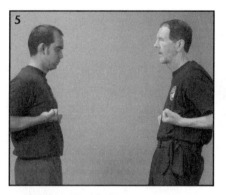

⋏Withdraw the blocking arm to chambered position.

⋏Now extend the right palm-up block using forward pressure.

⋏Snap arm down into a palm-down block.

⋏Return arm to palm-up block. Execute the drill in a 1-2-3 rhythm. Practice in cycles of 10 reps on each side.

Blocking Drill No. 2

⋏Starting position.

⋏Begin with left palm-up block, blocking with the inside of forearm.

⋏Drop the wrist and block with a low Wing Block.

⋏Return to left inside palm-up block.

⋀Withdraw arm.

⋀Repeat palm-up block with right hand.

⋀Drop wrist and block with low
Wing Block.

⋀Return to palm-up block. As with
Blocking Exercise No. 1, practice in
cycles of up to 10 reps on each side.

Blocking Drill No. 3

⚘ Ready position.

⚘ Block with double "scissors" block, left hand down, right palm-up, blocking at the wrists.

⚘ Now block with double "scissors" block, right hand down, left hand palm-up, blocking at the wrists.

⚘ Continue blocking left and right sides in cycles of ten. Remember to maintain forward pressure in the arms as you make contact.

Blocking Drill No. 4

⅄ Ready position.

⅄ Block with left high palm-up block and right low Wing Block. Again, contact should be made at the wrists using forward energy.

⅄ Block with right high palm-up block and left low Wing Block.

⅄ Continuing blocking left and right sides in cycles of ten. Maintain forward pressure! A maxim in Wing Chun states "all strikes can be blocks and all blocks can be strikes." So maintaining forward pressure is very important in all blocking exercises.

The Four Gates

[The dotted lines define the four basic "upper gates." The gates are defined by the vertical "midline," and horizontal "elbow line."]

Solo Blocking Drill No. 1

⋏Assume basic Wing Chun square stance.

⋏Raise the left hand into palm-up block.

⋏Sweep arm down into a downward block.

⋏ Return arm to palm-up position.

⋏ Pull back left hand.

⋏ Raise the right hand into palm-up block.

⋏ Sweep arm down into a downward block.

⋏ Raise the right hand into palm-up block.

⋏ Return to basic stance by pulling back right arm.

Solo Blocking Drill No. 2

◁ Basic stance.

➢ Rotate the left palm into the center. Execute a palm-up elbow block, blocking to the inside.

◁ Drop elbow to the outside to execute a low Wing Block.

➢ Rotate arm back into the palm-up block.

⋏Return to basic stance.

⋏Rotate the right palm into the center. Execute a palm-up elbow block, blocking to the inside.

⋏Drop elbow to the outside to execute a low Wing Block.

⋏Rotate arm back into the palm-up block position.

⋏Return to basic stance.

Solo Blocking Drill No. 3—Double Block

◄ Basic stance.

➤ Begin by sweeping across the body with left palm-up and right palm-down "scissors" block.

◄ Sweep hands across the body.

➤ Snap into right side "scissors" block.

◁ Sweep arms across body.

▷ Repeat previous block on left side. Practice blocks by continuously blocking left and right sides.

◁ Return to basic stance.

Solo Blocking Drill No. 4

◁ Basic stance.

➢ Raise left hand in a palm-up block. Rotate right hand into a low Wing Block.

◁ Rotate right arm on the inside into right palm-up block and lower arm into a left low Wing Block.

➢ Completed position.

◄Again, rotate left arm into left palm-up block and right low Wing Block.

➤Completed position.

◄Return to basic stance.

Simultaneous Block and Punch Drill

◄ From the parallel stance, execute a left palm-up block and simultaneous straight punch.

◄ Switch to right side with right palm-up block and a simultaneous left punch.

◁ Block down with the left arm and right simultaneous punch.

➢ Sweep down with the right downward block and simultaneous left punch.

◁ Return to basic position.

Protecting the Four Gates from a Pivoting Stance

◁ Protecting left upper gate with simultaneous block-punch.

◁ Protecting right upper gate with simultaneous block-punch.

◄Protecting left lower gate with simultaneous block-punch.

►Protecting right lower gate with simultaneous block-punch.

◄Return to basic position with simultaneous block-punch.

Protecting the Four Gates from a Fighting Stance

◄ Assume a left guarding stance.

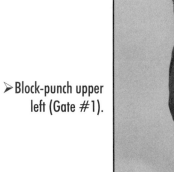

➢ Block-punch upper left (Gate #1).

◄ Block-punch upper right (Gate #2).

➢ Block-punch lower left (Gate #3).

⋏Block-punch lower right
(Gate #4).

⋏Assume a right side
guarding stance.

⋏Block-punch upper right
(Gate #1).

⋏Block-punch upper left
(Gate #2).

⋏Block-punch lower right
(Gate #3).

⋏Block-punch lower left
(Gate #4).

Pak Sau

"Pak Sau" is the term given by the Chinese for the Wing Chun "Slapping Block." "Pak Da," which means to simultaneously hit as you block, refers to the slap hand block and simultaneous strike combinations. Pak Sau is one of the most functional blocks in Kung-Fu, and variations of it can be seen throughout both Karate and western boxing. I believe this to be the first time that all of the basic ten Pak Da entries have been shown in one volume. There are other variations but these are the ten major entries used in Wing Chun to quickly close in on an opponent.

The Ten Major "Pak Da" entries

1. Pak Sau No. 1—Basic Entry
2. Pak Sau No. 2—Lin Lap Sau
3. Pak Sau No. 3—Elbow Rollover
4. Pak Sau No. 4—Heun Sau
5. Pak Sau No. 5—Double Pak
6. Pak Sau No. 6—Tan Lap Sau
7. Pak Sau No. 7—Noy Bong Sau
8. Pak Sau No. 8—Outer Gate Punch
9. Pak Sau No. 9—Double Palm Press
10. Pak Sau No. 10—Inside Lap Sau

"Pak Da" is one of the most effective means of safely attacking or countering an opponent's hands. If you can execute a "Pak Da" correctly, it will lead you into "trapping."

Pak Sau/Pak Da

[Only the right side "Pak Da" drills are shown. However, all techniques should be practiced on left and right sides. You must be "double-sided" in Wing Chun—able to attack or protect yourself with either hand.

Pak Sau Drill No. 1

◄ Sifu Lamb and Quang begin the "Pak Da" exercises by assuming a "crossed bridge" or forward fighting position.

◄Sifu Lamb begins the drill by slapping down into Quang's lead arm and prepares to punch with the right hand.

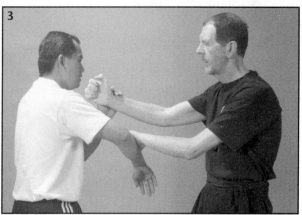

◄Quang's response is to protect himself with a left slap block and, simultaneously, he allows his lead arm to collapse into a low Wing Block to receive Sifu Lamb's forward energy as he slap blocks the right punch.

◄Sifu Lamb and Quang return to the right "crossed bridge" position.

◁ Now Quang attacks and Sifu Lamb protects with the left slap block and low Wing Block. From now on all entries will show only Sifu Lamb attacking. However, in practice, both partners must practice both attack and defense.

Pak Sau Drill No. 2

◁ "Crossed bridge" position.

◁ Sifu Lamb attacks. As before Quang protects himself with a left slap block and low Right Wing Block.

◁ Sifu Lamb switches his left slapping hand into a grab and pulls down on Quang's left arm at the same time. Sifu Lamb then re-chambers his right hand for a second attack.

◄Sifu Lamb re-attacks for Quang's neck with a sweeping knife hand strike.

◄Return to "crossed bridge" position.

Pak Sau Drill No. 3

◄ "Crossed bridge" position.

◄ Sifu Lamb attacks. Quang protects as before.

◄ This time, Sifu Lamb allows his punching hand to collapse.

◄Sifu Lamb rolls his right elbow over Quang's blocking hand.

◄In one fluid motion, Sifu Lamb continues to roll his arm into a vertical backfist strike.

◄Return to "crossed bridge" position.

Pak Sau Drill No. 4

◄ "Crossed bridge" position.

◄ Sifu Lamb attacks. Quang defends as before.

◄ Sifu Lamb circles his right hand around Quang's left block, pressing forward.

◁ Now Sifu Lamb pins Quang's arms and prepares to punch.

◁ Sifu Lamb simultaneously blocks and strikes Quang with a left punch.

◁ Return to "crossed bridge" position.

Pak Sau Drill No. 5

◄ "Crossed bridge" position.

◄ Sifu Lamb attacks.
Quang defends.

◁Sifu Lamb slap blocks Quang's blocking hand and continues his attack with the right hand, switching from a punch to a side palm attack for the jaw.

◁Return to "crossed bridge" position.

Pak Sau Drill No. 6

◄ "Crossed bridge" position.

◄ Sifu Lamb attacks.
Quang defends.

◄ Sifu Lamb presses his
palm-up block against
Quang's wrist, breaking
Quang's grasp.

⋏The palm-up block thrusts forward
and extends into a palm-up finger jab.

⋏Sifu Lamb sinks his elbow to trap
Quang's arms.

⋏Sifu Lamb pulls down on Quang's arms,
executing a grab, press, and punch to finish
the technique.

⋏Return to "crossed bridge" position.

Pak Sau Drill No. 7

◁ "Crossed bridge" position.

◁ Sifu Lamb attacks.
Quang defends.

◁ Sifu Lamb converts
his punching hand into
a downward reverse
Wing Block pin position.

◁ Continuing to control Quang's elbow, Sifu Lamb strikes with a left punch to the head.

◁ Return to "crossed bridge" position.

Pak Sau Drill No. 8

◄ "Crossed bridge" position.

◄ Sifu Lamb "block-hits" Quang's guarding hand using an "outer gate" punch.

◄ With a "sawing" motion, Sifu Lamb withdraws his left arm down Quang's forearm, turning his punch into a slap block.

◁ Lamb finishes with a "press"-punch combination attack.

◁ Return to "crossed bridge" position.

Pak Sau Drill No. 9

◄ "Crossed bridge" position.

◄ Sifu Lamb attacks.
Quang defends.

◄ Sifu Lamb traps
Quang's arms with a
left "grabbing" hand.

◁ Lamb presses with both palms to compress Quang's forearms, effecting a pin.

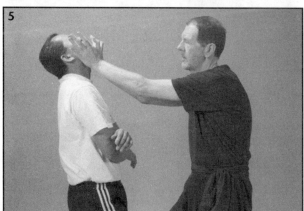

◁ Sifu Lamb finishes with a double palm attack to Quang's head.

◁ Return to "crossed bridge" position.

Pak Sau Drill No. 10

◄ "Crossed bridge" position.

◄ Sifu Lamb attacks.
Quang defends.

◄ Sifu Lamb pulls down
with his right hand against
Quang's block.

◁Lamb finishes with an inside grab-punch combination.

◁Return to "crossed bridge" position.

Trapping

Wing Chun trapping skills are unique in the martial arts. Trapping is the art of pinning or obstructing an attacker's potential line of attack. To be effective, traps need to be adaptable and flexible in nature. Some traps depend upon an attacker using excessive "holding. But if the attacker releases his grip and reattacks, you must be able to adapt to the new situation that this creates. Therefore, the concept of trapping or pinning an attacker's hand is built right into the Wing Chun system.

Here are three examples of trapping techniques.

1. Trapping from the Quan Sau position
2. Lin Lap trap
3. Double Lap Sau trap

Nos. 2 and 3 are variations from the previously shown Pak Da entry No. 2.

Trap No. 1

ꕔ Sifu Lamb and Ryan begin with a "crossed bridge" position.

ꕔ Ryan pulls down Sifu Lamb's guarding hand and executes a left punch.

⋏Sifu Lamb responds with a high palm-up block and low right Wing Block.

⋏Sifu Lamb crosses Ryan's hands to effect a trap by pulling down on the left arm.

⋏Ryan releases his grip on Sifu Lamb's right wrist to prevent his arms from being pinned.

⋏Sensing the change in energy flow and direction, Sifu Lamb pushes Ryan's left arm straight back to keep the right arm pinned. This move completes the trap.

Trap No. 2

⋏ Sifu Lamb faces Quang in the "crossed bridge" position.

⋏ Sifu Lamb executes a left slap block and right straight punch combination. Quang protects with a left slap block.

⋏ Sifu Lamb pulls down Quang's blocking hand and attempts a pin. Anticipating Sifu Lamb's intentions, Quang tries to bring his right hand up the middle for protection.

⋏ Sifu Lamb slides in with a double palm press to effect a trap, effectively pinning Quang's arms.

Trap No. 3

◁ "Crossed bridge" position.

◁ Sifu Lamb attacks with classic Pak Da entry. Quang responds with high slap block and low Wing Block.

◁ Sifu Lamb slides his left arm behind Quang's left arm to prepare for a grab-punch technique.

◁ Sifu Lamb grabs Quang's hand.

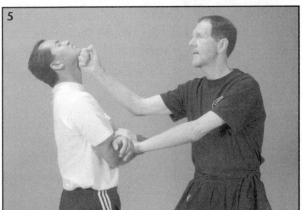

◁ Sifu Lamb executes a punch and pin.

◁ Quang struggles to free his arms.

⋏Sensing the change in energy and direction, Sifu Lamb executes a left suppression punch to control Quang's leading arm.

⋏Sifu Lamb reaches across to pin Quang's arms and strikes again.

⋏Sifu Lamb circles and pins Quang's arms in a double trap.

⋏A finishing blow is applied to the head as Sifu Lamb maintains the trap and pins with his right hand.

Miscellaneous Trapping Example

◄Sifu Lamb faces Ryan in the "crossed bridge" position.

◄Sifu Lamb attacks, Ryan protects.

◄Sifu Lamb applies a palm-up block to dislodge Ryan's slap block.

◁ Sifu Lamb applies a grab, trapping Ryan's hand.

◁ Sifu Lamb applies a finishing strike.

◁ Ryan breaks out of the trap and attacks with a right punch and left hand control.

⋏Sifu Lamb protects with a "Quan Sau" block.

⋏Lamb grabs the inside of Ryan's right arm.

⋏Sifu Lamb traps Ryan's arms and sets up for a left counter-punch.

⋏While maintaining the trap, Lamb applies a finishing blow.

Lap Sau

Lap Sau or "Grabbing Hand" is one of the most basic training drills in Wing Chun. It has many variations but, basically, it combines three major techniques, wing Block, grab, and punch, then recycles them in a continuous reciprocal exercise designed to get the techniques "hard wired" into the subconscious mind. It is said of Lap Sau that, only when it is "in your bones" can it be used effectively for self-defense.

In the beginning Lap Sau is performed from a square position. However, when used in combat it is usually done with a body shift to avoid being hit by a bigger or stronger opponent. To be effective, techniques must be soft and flexible, but explosive.

Basic Lap Sau Drill
1. Wing Block Defense
2. Grabbing attacker's arm
3. Counter Punch
4. Partner repeats the sequence on the opposite side.

◄Sifu Lamb controls Ryan's hands.

◄Sifu Lamb pulls Ryan's arm down and punches.

◄Ryan protects with a wing block.

◁ Ryan counter-punches.

◁ Sifu Lamb responds with a wing block.

◁ Sifu Lamb grabs and counter-punches.

◁ Ryan responds with a wing block.

◁ Ryan changes his wing block to a palm-up block punching with opposite hand.

◁ This sets drill up on opposite side.

The Concept of Flow

In Wing Chun to "flow" is to have the ability to follow up with an immediate counter technique or movement if your present line of attack has been stopped. "Flowing" means being able to transition seamlessly from attack to defense, and vice versa. It means not being "fixed," but being free to penetrate whenever you find a hole in your opponent's defenses. It also means being able to keep the pressure on until you overwhelm your opponent. When "flowing," all techniques should be steady and controlled. To use an analogy, if you were hitting a nail with a hammer, you would not use one hundred percent of your strength on the first blow. Rather, you would gradually increase the pressure until you were sure that your final blow would drive the nail home. Correct flow in Wing Chun can only be learned from an experienced teacher, through the medium of Chi Sau or "Sticking Hands," which is based on the concept of Yin and Yang, and is the life blood of Wing Chun Kung-Fu. The following photos illustrate the concepts that are learned through Chi Sau.

◄Basic chi sau positions.

◄Basic rolling-positions reversed.

◄Sifu Lamb rolls Ryan's hands to the outside.

◄ Ryan attempts to slip over Sifu Lamb's wing block.

◄ Sifu Lamb gains control through using a double wing block and palm-up block control.

◄ Sifu Lamb continues to roll.

◄ Sifu Lamb uses inside and outside control.

◄ Ryan senses a hole and attempts a slap-block attack.

◄ Sifu Lamb deflects the attack.

◁Sifu Lamb regains control.

◁And back to basic rolling.

Self-Defense Applications

Studying Kung-Fu is hard work, but training with partners can be a lot of fun. However, one should not lose sight of the fact that the martial arts were developed primarily as a means of self-defense. Physical conditioning and mental enlightenment are bonuses to martial arts training. But the bottom line is being able to use the skills you have learned to save your neck in a street confrontation. If you are attacked and you cannot escape, you must stand your ground and counterattack with as much aggression as possible. You must try to take the initiative away from your attacker or attackers, especially if they are armed. Remember, on the street you are dealing with ruthless people who will not give you a second chance. So when your life depends upon it, "Hit hard and hit first!" If someone is attacking you with deadly force, then you must counter with the same amount of force. You must "do unto others before they do unto you!" Be explosive!

The following photos illustrate a variety of self-defense situations and their possible Wing Chun counters.

Attack No. 1—The Straight Punch

◄ Sifu Lamb deflects the straight punch.

◄ He controls Ryan's punching arm.

◄ Then pulls Ryan into a body front kick.

Attack No. 2—The Grab

⋏Sifu Lamb deflects Ryan's grab attempt.

⋏Sifu Lamb applies a front kick counter.

⋏Sifu Lamb reverses Ryan's grab.

⋏Elbow finishing strike.

Attack No. 3—The Front Kick

◄ Sifu Lamb deflects Ryan's front kick with an inside leg block.

◄ He counter kicks with a low side kick.

Attack No. 4—The Round Kick

◁ Ryan sets up for a round kick.

◁ In one motion Sifu Lamb blocks Ryan's kick and counter kicks.

Attack No. 5—The Side Kick

⋏ Ryan begins a side kick attack.

⋏ Sifu Lamb applies a strong forearm block.

⋏ Sifu Lamb deflects Ryan's leg to the side.

⋏ He steps in to knock Ryan over and off his base leg.

CONCLUSION

If, like me, the art of Wing Chun excites you, then I hope you have enjoyed this book. In Volume two, I plan to demonstrate Chi Sau and counter trapping techniques and, for the first time, present all three Wing Chun sets in one comprehensive volume.

I look forward to seeing you again in Volume two of "Explosive" Combat Wing Chun.

—